IMAGES
of England

ALCESTER

Alfred Crouch, outside his shop at 3 Swan Street.

IMAGES
of England

ALCESTER

Compiled by
Melvyn Amos

TEMPUS

First published 1998
Reprinted 2000
Copyright © Melvyn Amos, 1998

Tempus Publishing Limited
The Mill, Brimscombe Port,
Stroud, Gloucestershire, GL5 2QG

ISBN 0 7524 1170 5

Typesetting and origination by
Tempus Publishing Limited
Printed in Great Britain by
Midway Clark Printing, Wiltshire

An early Foden steam wagon with steel wheels, tyres and brake blocks, *c.* 1905.

Contents

A pig roast towards the foot of Bleachfield Street, in 1935.

Introduction

The publication of this book marks my twenty-fifth year of working in Alcester. It was in 1973 that I joined Allan Everatt as an assistant solicitor, shortly after he had moved premises to 19 Church Street. He had recently acquired the part time practice of Whiteley & Pickering which had run on the basis of two daily visits per week by my old friend and mentor Brian Prescott.

Allan had originally also bought the practice of W.H. Scott which had operated for many years from premises in Henley Street. He inherited piles of old papers and documents which he could do no more than transfer without inspection to the cellar at Church Street. One of my first tasks was to organize some permanent and proper storage facility within that cellar which meant that I had to dispose of a vast amount of paperwork, much of which was mildewed and decaying. Fortunately, I had long since recognized the potential importance of old documentation through my interest in the collection of old postcards of Redditch and it was therefore with care that I approached the job in hand, rescuing so far as possible all old title deeds, wills, probates and other papers which touched upon any aspect of the history of Alcester. My firm was in this way able to make available to the Local Historical Society, items which would assist Edward Saville in the compilation of his many occasional papers which are recommended to the reader and are available at Alcester Library.

Over my years in practice, I have also taken the opportunity of gleaning, from the various sets of deeds which have passed through my hands, further information concerning local properties. Along with the memories of a number of older residents, this has assisted me greatly in preparation of the captions to the various pictures which appear within. It must be stressed that this is not a history book – it is intended for entertainment. Memories are often unreliable, documents are not always entirely complete and accordingly apologies are given in advance for any inaccuracies which may appear.

A question often raised is: why are there so many photographs available dating from the early years of this century? The answer lies in the history of the postcard. Until 1902, only the name and address of the person to whom the postcard was being sent could be written on the stamped side of the card. The message, along with any picture had to appear on the front and consequently very early cards were restricted in content, having to rely on much reduced printed views. From 1902, when the regulations altered allowing the address and message to appear in the same side, real photographs were printed with postcard backs. They were used by the population in the same way that we use the telephone today, particularly as cards posted early morning could be expected to be delivered later the same day.

So far as postcards are concerned, there are two photographers of importance to Alcester, both of whom operated from the same premises at 45 High Street. Before the First World War, Lewis Brothers of Redditch produced sepia photographs of Alcester, initially opening their Alcester premises each Wednesday. To help further with identification, their cards were usually captioned and numbered in freehand with a dot either side of the number. I have seen numbers up to ninety-nine with a further set of six for Ragley Hall. Incidentally, postcards were almost always sold by the half-dozen which can help a collector aiming for a full set of, for example, Alcester Peace Pageant. The other photographer of importance was W.H. Smith and his postcards often bore his initials or were printed with a white border surround. These were produced later than the Lewis Brothers, from about 1914 to the Second World War.

Finally, while this book contains the usual acknowledgements may I extend special recognition and thanks to Dilys Ross for her general assistance and for the time which she has spent in the compiling of material and information, together with the most important task of the final proof reading.

Melvyn Amos
May 1998

One

Evesham Street
and Arrow

A convenient focal point for our photographic journey around the town is the junction of the roads from Redditch, Evesham and Stratford-upon-Avon. We can immediately see the significance of the Globe sculpture standing on the traffic island today. The Globe Inn, which was originally built around 1775, was a coaching inn during the nineteenth century and later catered for commercial travellers; it was known between the wars as the Globe Hotel, selling Atkinsons Aston Ales. When motor traffic became heavier this junction was regarded as dangerous, as the turn for Redditch, from the Evesham direction in particular, was blind. There would often be a policeman on point duty at the junction and by the mid 1960s, when the building was demolished, the speed of traffic from Redditch travelling to Stratford-upon-Avon had significantly increased the risk of accident. To the left can be seen Hodge's Bakery, part of one of Alcester's finest timber-framed properties, which was lost to the town in the late 1950s. The business specialized in party catering and celebratory cakes, but also had a traditional tea shop. Alcester Co-op later took over the shop for the sale of products from its bakehouse which is located to the rear of the shop premises which can be seen in the background in Evesham Street.

The premises of Alcester Co-operative Society Limited dominate this end of Evesham Street. The two cottages to the right were later used as offices by the Co-op, but at this time No. 1 is advertising sewing machines for sale. The first two properties to the left were later occupied by the Co-op as their confectionery and butchers' shops respectively and the slaughter house was located to the rear. Note the original clock which was later replaced with a commemorative octagonal design.

The Rose and Crown was a pub until the late 1960s. The Bell opposite was, for a short time in its history, known as the Blue Bell. The advertisement on the wall of The Bell is for Alcester Old Boys football club.

In the year 1591, Walter Newport bequeathed an endowment to provide a school, 'for the teaching of poor men's children at Alcester.' It is, however, likely that the money benefited a school that had already been in existence since around 1490, and was run in the Chantry of Our Lady by a chantry priest. The original endowment was £20 per year, which clearly became insufficient to maintain the school as the years passed. It eventually became necessary to take in paying boarders and the attic rooms were used as dormitories. The original name of Newport's Free School would change to become a grammar school in the traditional sense as the number of boarding children increased. A new school opened on Birmingham Road in 1912, and the old stone buildings pictured below became used as three separate dwellings. Sadly they were demolished in the 1960s to make way for Wimpey's first development in the town. The school was approached by way of a footpath continuing from Birch Abbey Lane and also by a track from Bleachfield Street. As there is no indication to any possible connection with an Abbey, it is considered highly likely that the road name Birch Abbey originated from a satirical name given to the school itself, bearing in mind that corporal punishment was an everyday occurrence.

The two houses forming the taller building at the corner of Birch Abbey shared a common courtyard with five other houses. This was a common arrangement for properties constructed in the early nineteenth century and the courtyard would provide a shared water supply with very basic wash house and toilet facilities. Although all of the houses are completely self-contained today, the deeds still provide for common use and maintenance of the courtyard.

The original White Lion stood on Evesham Street. A new public house, bearing the same name was built in the late 1930s, although it was positioned further back than the original.

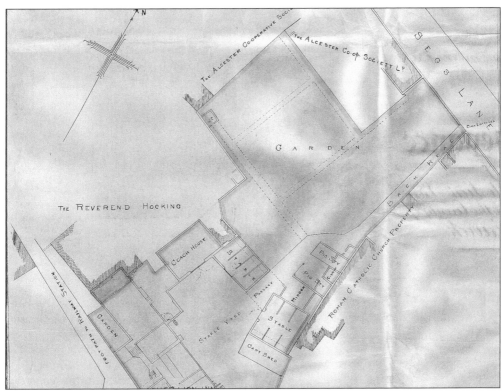

This plan is taken from a deed dated 29 September 1897, by which the White Lion was sold to a Leamington brewery company, Lucas & Co. Ltd by the executor of George Millington's will, at a price of £1,400. George Millington had been licensee from 1883. The ample stabling would suggest considerable business in the letting of rooms. The land to the east side is marked as Roman Catholic church property and was the site of a perry mill with two cottages fronting to Evesham Street, which have long since been demolished. Lucas & Co. Ltd bought this site in 1936 when the vendors are specifically described as the Trustees of Douai Abbey, Woolhampton, Berkshire. Lucas & Co. Ltd owned various other licensed premises in the town from time to time including The Bear.

Frank Stiles, who has been described to me as a very well respected man, was licensee from 1905 until 1932.

Poplar Cottage was a private girls' school for much of the nineteenth century. Note that the window immediately above the front door was actually bricked in to save on window tax. The building to the side was added as the school expanded and is now a separate house. William and Martha Facer lived here at the time when the photograph was taken. They were staunch Methodists, who donated the organ to the original Methodist chapel on Priory Road. William and his brother Joseph Facer were tailors from Stratford.

The road leaves Alcester for Arrow and to the right can be seen the entrance to Acorn House. This was occupied for a long time by local doctors and used as their surgery, until the opening of Priory Clinic.

In the garden to this property (blighted by the by-pass but now lived in again) sits the Arrow Waterwheel. In the 1870s, the wheel helped to provide Alcester with its first mains water supply by pumping water up to a reservoir from which it ran, by gravity, into the town.

The tollhouse at the junction with Arrow Lane was built in 1826. The blocks of cottages are seventeenth-century timber-framed properties, but brick infilling has replaced the original wattle and daub. The village school, which closed in 1928, can be seen behind the tollhouse and the schoolmaster lived in the centre of the three cottages covered with vine.

Multi-view postcards were a popular novelty; the local photographer used four or five negatives from stock. This one commemorates the retirement of Reverend Beauchamp Stannus at the age of 86. He was a descendant through his mother's side of the Conway family and regularly attacked the Catholic church in his parish magazine.

The unveiling ceremony of the Arrow War Memorial for the men from the 'Parish of Arrow who gave their lives for justice and freedom in the Great War, 1914–1918.'

Two

Swan Street and Stratford Road

Until about 1870, Swan Street was called Huckerhurst Street and for a short period around the turn of the century, Bleachfield Street was known as Regent Street. Holding a prominent postion in the shops along the north side of Swan Street are the premises of Thomas Court, watchmaker, jeweller, and supplier of 'spectacles to suit all sights'. The premises later became a bicycle shop. Burdett's sold goods from the bakery of William Burdett attached to 9 Church Street. Shepherd's Boot Warehouse was a general clothier's, tailor's, outfitter's and hatter's, as well as housing the town library from 1954–1968. The next buildings formed three shops, the first and second were owned by William Devey and his wife who ran a fishmonger's and greengrocer's, and the third was owned by A.H. Crouch, who ran a tobacconist. This building has of course now been demolished, along with those on the south side of Swan Street, and has been replaced by the present and unimaginative flat roofed buildings.

The Swan was an important coaching inn during the eighteenth century, where coaches stopped on the journey from London to Holyhead, and other cross country routes. Later, travelling trade was reduced to more local destinations, such as Birmingham and Leamington Spa. The inn was also the meeting place for a number of local organizations, such as the Masons and Foresters. The building that is now Lloyds Bank was originally opened in the 1880s as the Gloucester Banking Company and was later the premises of Capital and Counties Bank. In those days the bank manager was required to live over the premises, and the last manager to do this was Paul Mackintosh.

Staff at the Alcester Cycle Company with the Speedwell bicycle. In 1903, the business was transferred from Priory Road to the Abbey Works on Bleachfield Street and they later manufactured side cars for motor cycle manufacturers, including Harley Davidson. Workers at shops and factories were quite happy to pose for the photographer, making a welcome break in what would have been a very long working day. Such pictures are much sought after by postcard collectors and command high prices due to their social history interest.

The prominent sign for the Dog and Partridge is still in position today but in the background we can also see the New Inn, although some two hundred years ago it was named the Cock and Breeches. Many of the dwellings in Bleachfield Street were occupied by needle workers, as there had formerly been a fairly substantial needle factory on the site later occupied by Baromix.

This picture could just as well be captioned 'The Flood at Alcester on 10 April 1998', such is the similarity of the scenes in the town on the morning of that day. The storm in 1924 started at about six o'clock on the evening of 31 May and raged all night, causing severe flooding throughout the town. Note also the Cross Keys public house which was formed from the last two of a row of seven cottages. This was formerly known as the Crosswells Inn, until a full licence was granted in 1904, when the Three Tuns was closing.

Mary Helen Tarver, at her home in The Rookery. She is holding one of her sons David with another son Charles standing beside her.

These cottages in Stratford Road, together with the Great House in Gas House Lane, occupied the land facing the Cross Keys. Together, they became the Parish Workhouse or Poor House during the eighteenth century and remained as such until 1834. By the time of this photograph there were seventeen separate dwellings collectively known as The Rookery. They were described to me as 'disgusting slums', and all of them were demolished around 1956.

STRATFORD RD ALCESTER

A detailed view of the first properties built in Alcester from the Stratford direction, around 1930. Four more old cottages can be seen to the side of The Rookery. The railings outside Nos. 44–50 were removed in aid of the war effort. William Smallwood provided money to build the Alms House on Birmingham Road, and lived at Stratford House to the left for at least twenty years prior to his death in 1901. A district of Redditch and the town's hospital were named after his family.

A visit to the local recreation ground would have been regarded as a relatively formal affair with the children dressed accordingly in coats or jackets with flat hats. The course of the river has changed since this picture which was taken between the wars.

Oversley Bridge was in constant need of repair, which had to be paid for through local taxes until the road from Stratford was turnpiked in 1754. The turnpike trust held its meetings at The Angel, in Church Street. Looking back at the town from this point the most obvious alteration to the skyline is the new Corinthian Court development which now replaces the view of Stratford House.

There are several consecutively numbered views of Oversley taken by Lewis around 1906; these probably number twelve in all, as postcards were usually sold by the half-dozen. Local inhabitants, particularly children, were eager to pose for the photographer.

This couple also appear in the previous photograph and indeed in a number of others which were clearly taken on the same day. In all likelihood this is one of the Lewis brothers and his wife looking to add a human touch to what would otherwise be an uninteresting subject.

The Tarver family's annual Easter picnic on Primrose Hill. Mary Helen, who we saw at the Rookery, is fourth from right holding Louisa Jane, and the three boys to the front are Arthur, Dick and Joe. The family still live locally and the photograph has been passed among its many members.

The River Alne at Hoo Mill was also known as the Hoo Stream, 'hoo' being an old English word meaning 'bank'. The mill itself was originally a corn mill and later used for the pointing of needles. It is now a cider mill.

Three

Priory Road and Birmingham Road

The Benedictine Monastery was founded by Ralph Boteler, Lord of Oversley in 1140, and occupied the site behind the present grammar school. Hence, the route from the town to the monastery was originally known as Abbey Street. By the end of the seventeenth century, the Abbey had been reduced to a Priory, so the documents dating from then refer to Priory Street or Priory Lane and the northern section would have been called Birmingham Road after the railway came to town. Guyvers Garage can be seen just behind The Globe Inn and the open stretch to the rear of that was for many years Alcester's cattle market. It was given to the town by the then Marquess of Hertford in 1872, to replace the similar market which had been held in the High Street. The jeweller's at the junction with Swan Street became Godfrey's cycle shop. This use continued for many years, and was later under the proprietorship of George Clark, a renowned coach builder with works at Arrow. Another of the buildings to the right still stands today, as an estate agent's and the original Methodist chapel can be seen literally supported by the premises on either side. This support was necessary as it was built in 1872 with only a single brick skin. When the cottages to the north side were demolished, the chapel was in danger of collapse and Alcester Builders were called on to provide metal strapping which prolonged its life. The old chapel could not however survive the pulling down of the property on the other side in 1966. This was the second chapel to occupy the site as there had been an earlier chapel dating from 1812, when the land was given to the Trustees by Henry Nash of Haselor.

Now a private house, the Golden Lion was run as a pub selling beer and cider only, from about 1850 until it closed in 1935.

The schoolroom this side of the Lord Nelson public house, was used as a Sunday school until 1911, then as a handicraft centre for local schools until 1952. Around 1908, when this picture was taken, the entrance to the Lord Nelson was on Priory Road itself rather than at the side as is the case today. There was no traditional pub sign at the Lord Nelson at this time.

Built in 1889, at a cost of £2,000, the Roman Catholic church stands on land bought from Lord Hertford. The school building opened in 1902, and was open to all ages until 1961, when the seniors were transferred to St Bede's, in Redditch. The infants and juniors continued to study here until moving to the new building in St Faith's Road in 1965.

Contrast the ornate interior of the Catholic church as shown in this picture taken in the early years of this century with the very plain interior of the church as it is today. The statuettes represent the Stations of the Cross.

Gresley House, on the left, which was earlier known as Milford House, was the home of the local Baptist minister for several decades during the nineteenth century. The Priory, to the right, was built around 1830, as a private house. During the 1850s however, a needle factory which employed a number of local men and children, was set up to the rear of the building. By 1890 the Priory Works were manufacturing bicycles, although they reverted to being a needlework factory in 1903. A flock of sheep can be seen coming from the market in the background and the handcart is that of Cockerton's Bakery.

In 1855, a new cemetery was opened in a field known as Hither Mill Close which had been donated by Lord Hertford. The chapel seen in the picture was originally consecrated in 1861, although this was demolished in 1963. The first site had to be extended when it became full.

The Midland Loop was a railway line linking Redditch with Evesham, to give access from the Vale of Evesham to the northern industrial towns and Bristol and Gloucester docks. Alcester station opened in 1866, and the line from Evesham was extended to Redditch two years later. Midland Railway quickly took over the Evesham & Redditch Railway Company and one of its locomotives can be seen here entering the station. The signalman seems more intent on the camera, which is a little worrying. The line, which provided a route to London connecting at Bearley, was opened as the Alcester Railway in 1876. It was however, soon taken over by Great Western Railway. Many of the routes taken by the two lines are still clear today, particularly the road bridges and girder bridge over the river behind the Roebuck pub. However, much of the land has since been bought to extend gardens, notably to the houses in Roebuck Park and Roman Way. The importance of the railway to the town cannot be over estimated. It was a particular boost for the needle trade as it meant that coal could be brought in, whereas horse wagons had previously had to travel from the canal at Tardebigge. Day trips to such places as the Lickey Hills or even the seaside now became possible. Unfortunately, passenger services ceased in 1962, mainly due to the dangerous state of the tunnel at Redditch.

The message on the back of this card reads, 'the place we did not stop at, nor did we want to on August 26 1916'. In the picture we can see the chapel and the gravestones which were destroyed in 1981. Although the parish church obtained the appropriate legal authority, the demolition caused much distress to many local people. It may even be possible that this site could be built upon in future years.

In the foreground we see Nos. 26 and 28 Birmingham Road, although the deeds clearly indicate this to have been the public house known as The Mug House. The sign above the door to No. 28 is for Harry Pritchard, a shoe repairer, who was also, for a time, Alcester's town crier. The next four properties are almshouses built in 1659, by John Bridges to be occupied by four poor women. The message on this card tells that the cross marks the position of a school camp which was held for children from the London area during the Second World War.

Four
High Street

ALCESTER .31.

The lower end of High Street was originally a bull ring where animals were baited. The road led up to the sheep market or beast market where animals were still being sold until 1872 and finally, to the Shambles, where butchers killed and sold their meat. We start with a lovely photograph by Lewis showing the range of shops up to Midland Bank; all of these are timber framed, although they do not appear to be. The corner shop has been called Whitehead's since the early 1870s, but was a grocer's for at least thirty years prior to that, run by Timms. Moving up the High Street we can see the long barber's pole at Hopkins, then Charles Freeman's 'the hygienic bakery' and restaurant, which later moved to other High Street premises.

This picture, taken some decades later, shows London House and Manchester House which are now clearly identified as such. The site of the Midland Bank has always been occupied by a bank, although the Midland itself is relatively new. It previously belonged to the Capital and Counties Bank, Metropolitan Bank and was originally Stourbridge & Kidderminster Bank. The manager's living accommodation was above the bank, in accordance with regulations, from around 1880.

The London House block, which is now the Unionist Club, was an eighteenth century addition to High Street. The café business had only recently opened when this photograph was taken. Prior to this, in the early 1920s, the premises were used by a nurseryman. Note the large gas lamp on the wall of the Royal Oak.

Church Parade Sept.er 12. 1915.

The delightful net curtains to the bank have gone but the gates are still there. What we now know as Lloyds Chemist, formerly Savory & Moore, can be seen as two separate shops. One was occupied by Burdett the grocer's and the other was a chemist called Adcock. The Adcock family were the chemists in the town for over one hundred years. They had operated from these premises since around 1887, and prior to that had owned a shop in Swan Street.

Earlier and later known as the Three Tuns, this property was from 1910 until 1963 the premises of William Hemming, painter and plumber. The Birmingham Midshires building society premises are seen here in their incarnation as a residence, although it had formerly been an inn known as The Talbot. Behind Hitching's ironmonger's shop was the Quaker Meeting House and this building also housed the offices of the local gas company from 1930–1970.

ALCESTER CHILDRENS OUTING SEPT 1ST 1928.

Our photographer must be on the upper floor of London House. As I know from personal experience, the sun beats into the properties on the west side of the High Street from early morning, hence the proliferation of blinds and sheets seen in the shop windows. The local Sunday schools usually organized children's outings at this time.

HIGH ST ALCESTER

WHSmith Photo 72

Next to Burdett's shop was the local reading room which later became a greengrocer's and fruiterer's run by the Baylis family for many years.

34

This earlier photograph shows London House before the café business was installed. In the foreground is the site now occupied by the second Lloyds chemist shop. This building previously housed the International Stores, which bought out George Mason, the grocer's. The grocer's at the time of this picture were known as Star Supply Stores and the butcher's shop belonged to the London Central Meat Co. Ltd, seen to the left. This butcher's later moved to 35a.

This is a picture of Lewis's shop at 45 High Street. A number of local view postcards can be seen in the shop window, as well as a selection of humorous cards and a notice saying 'Ministry Office for Servants'. In 1902, the Lewis Brothers were advertising that they were operating from High Street, Alcester on Wednesdays as photographers and picture frame makers, with frames made 'cheap and well'. The business was sold to W.H. Smith whose name can be seen on many later local photographs.

The Church Lads Brigade parading down the High Street past the premises of Averill, the rope maker's whose rope works and rope walk were behind No. 31. J.H. Sanders owned another butcher's shop and next door were the premises of Mabel Harris, a greengrocer. We then have a lodging house and the premises of Alcester Builders owned by the Buggins family from the turn of the century until 1968. As well as the rope works there was a malt house to the rear of these buildings. In those days many of the High Street properties had land extending to Moorfield Road.

The Bear was another coaching inn but coaches only stopped there on short distance routes. This was another pub which had been owned in the early years of the century by Lucas & Co. Limited. At this time, however, Ansells brewery had taken over and there was an off-licence with a separate entrance to the right of the main porch entrance.

This is the original stone clad Corn Exchange built in 1857. It was originally used for the buying and selling of goods but by the turn of the century it was used as a social centre and was let out for theatrical performances, concerts, temperance societies meetings and political assemblies, as well as being a venue for readings and lectures. Bioscopic pictures had been shown in the 1900s but it was not until 1924 that the Alcester Picture House opened in this building and the meetings and other activities were transferred to the Town Hall. It was known as the Regent until closing in 1961. The banners seen here are advertising the film *Sunny Side Up*, which was an early talking movie released in 1929. The building included a private house to the side which was demolished in 1965.

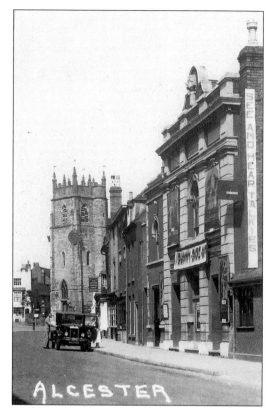

The Royal Warwickshire Regiment, parading along the High Street, around 1907. Deliveries are being made to William Breeze's grocery store and we can just see Herbert Crawford's, draper, upholsterer and cabinet maker to the left. Freeman's 'hygienic bakery' is at Nos. 12–14.

The baker's was that of George Fryer, in 1915. Barbon's fish and chip shop was then run by Mrs Williams, about whom all I can say is that she is recorded as having sold faggots and let her husband live in the wash-house! We can see two public houses, The Turk's Head and lower down, The Fox, which would have just closed at the time that this view was taken. Incidentally, a bakehouse, said to be from the Elizabethan period, was removed from the rear of No. 14 and is now on display at Avoncroft Museum of Buildings.

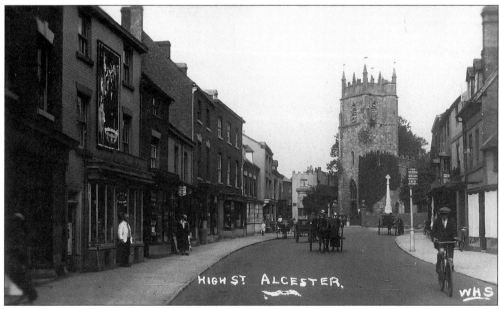

Mention should be made of the grocer William Breeze and the large advertisement for Bisto should be noted. Next door we have Thomas Dales' jeweller's and watch repairer's. The various carts in the picture appear to be for passengers and the practice of road users stopping in the middle of the High Street is one continued to this day.

No. 3, at the top of the High Street, can be seen in many old photographs with the name 'Blunn' over the door. Mrs Blunn ran a stationer's and fancy goods business, although, in more recent times it was an antique shop managed by Mrs Wilkes and is now a sports shop. Nos. 5 and 7 comprised a substantial grocery business for almost 200 years, run throughout that period by two families, the Jephcotts and the Buntings. No. 9 with the elegant bow fronted windows has, from time to time, been one or two separate shops with the tea rooms to the rear taking their name from the Tudor Rose design at the centre of the moulded ceiling. Vestiges of the sign for Hutton's fish and poultry shop can still be seen today.

In 1906, Henson's butcher's, who came from Stratford, bought No. 2 High Street, together with other land and property described as 'barns, slaughterhouse, stabling, shedding, piggeries, yard and garden'. Almost immediately a parcel of this land which fronted Gashouse Lane, formerly Coalbrook Lane, was sold off to the Alcester Gaslight Coal and Coke Company Limited. The shop manager's live-in quarters were to the left of the shop itself. Below the Turks Head, Bowen's drapery, which was run by the same family throughout this century, is seen to be named Victoria House.

39

From this earlier picture of Bunting's we can note that No. 9 is at this time occupied by Frank Sreeves, a carpenter. Lower down is an ironmongery business which was later run by the Stanley family.

Butter Street takes its name from the time when it was the site of a market for the sale of dairy produce. The narrowness of the street gave the storeholders some protection from the sunshine, and offered a cooler environment than that which would be found at other market sites, such as High Street or Henley Street. Here we see the rear of Nos. 2 and 4, with their windows wide open.

Five
Church Street and Henley Street

The first stretch of Church Street from High Street was known in medieval times as Shop Row, but the shops were actually on the church side of the street, probably more in the nature of stalls so that until about 1800 the street would still be quite narrow. Henley Street was also known as Sheep Street being at one time the site of a sheep market. Thomas Hunt, the naturalist, was also a taxidermist and was nicknamed by the youth of the town 'Hunt the Birdstuffer'. In his advertisement he described himself as a preserver of birds, animals, reptiles, fish, stag's heads, dogs, and foxes. He also advertised the selling of fancy skins for muffs, rugs and mats. There are a number of specimens of his work on display at Warwick Museum. The smaller ground floor window of the timber-framed building is that of my first office in the town. Hemmings the estate agents, which was formerly John Brown & Co. have been at No. 18 for many years but prior to that this site was occupied by the Electricity Service Centre at which many local people will recall paying their electricity bills.

Local societies would regularly march to church behind the town band and choir, attracting many spectators, including the little girl, Miss Barber, in the window of No. 10. We can clearly see Stanton's cycle shop, where Ben Barrow later had his antique's shop.

This is a Grade I listed building, said to date from around 1500. Looking down Malt Mill Lane it can be seen that the first story is jettied, although on Church Street the jetty has been underbuilt with brick and bay windows. Cycle repairs are offered, saying, 'ladies' and gentlemen's – orders promptly executed'. Most of the posters advertise railway trips to destinations such as Weston, Ilfracombe and Minehead. The horsedrawn coach may well be for the conveyance of passengers to the station.

Many years later the same building appears much tidier and there is now a sweet shop. The Royal Mail vans with GPO registrations indicate that there was a post office at No. 9, which was there from about 1865 until 1963. Solicitors have occupied No. 10 since the 1920s and many inhabitants will remember Jack Perry Plant.

John Wright was postmaster at the time of this photograph, in 1908. His family had once run a grocer's and baker's alongside the post office. However, by the early 1900s this space was needed by the post office to provide an increased number of services, including savings accounts, money orders, telegrams, annuities, and insurance. There were four deliveries of post each day with a delivery also being made on Christmas Day. Stamps were one penny for a letter and one half-penny for a postcard.

ST. NICHOLAS CHURCH, ALCESTER

An aerial view, in 1948. The main changes have been to the rear of the properties in Church

ARWICKSHIRE R·7819

Street and the High Street.

Ahead we see the bakery of James Fourt, which had earlier been a private school for boarders and day pupils. It is said that the building was once a hostelry known as the Golden Cup. The ivy-clad house with railings, to the right, is No. 8 Church Street, also known as Arrow House. It was lived in between the wars by George Thomas, the solicitor whose office was situated to the rear. At No. 7 The Limes, lived George Haines, whose father started Alcester Brewery at Church Street in the 1880s.

Oddly this postcard was published by a firm of photographers based entirely in the London area. Jim Adcock, the well known local chemist, lived at No. 6 during the 1930s and 1940s, but we should perhaps concentrate on Nos. 4 and 5 as this is historically, one of the most important buildings in the town, formerly The Angel Inn. There are many stories attached to the inn and the reader is referred to its history as written by Aubrey Gwynett, hopefully available from Alcester Library. Until it closed in 1865, the Assembly Room was housed in this building and many local groups met there.

In 1859, the Baptist chapel was built in front of the original 'Meeting House' under the ministry of the Reverend Moses Philpin. The railings were donated to the Second World War effort in 1942.

No prizes for spotting Miss Simpson who made all of her own hats and ran a milliner's called The Bonnet Box at No. 12 High Street. Mr Morris, the choirmaster, is to the left, and in the centre of the back row is William Burdett, who was a Sunday school teacher and superintendent for many years. The girl with glasses, in the front row, is Doris Payne.

Returning to Malt Mill Lane, this later view of the old Malt House shows the sweet shop opened by Bertha Stevens which was also known for selling unlawfully on Sundays. However, at the time of this picture the business was run by Albert Stevens. Next door is the antiques shop of Ben Barrow who moved from the High Street around 1934.

Malting was a most important industry to Alcester, and there were at least seven malt houses along Malt Mill Lane. The process involved keeping barley grain damp and warm until germination, which resulted in the starch being converted to sugar. Raising the temperature quickly kills the seedlings leaving the malt for use in the brewing process. There was an ample market in the town, as a number of the public houses brewed their own beer and up to the First World War; Alcester Brewery would have taken some of this supply, although it also operated its own malt house off Henley Street.

So far as possible the cottages along Malt Mill Lane have been restored to their original appearance in recent years, and now form part of a complex specifically designed to provide homes for elderly persons. A restored malt kiln can be found in the shared garden area.

Some of the residents of Malt Mill Lane in celebratory mood outside Grummett's shop which sold groceries, confectionery and newspapers.

There was no entrance to the Town Hall from this end as late as 1962, when this photograph was taken. It was originally built in 1618, as a market hall to provide shelter for corn sellers; the first storey was added some twenty-three years later.

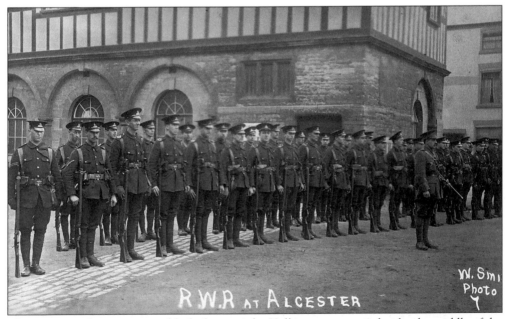

The townspeople were responsible for keeping the Hall in proper repair but by the middle of the nineteenth century, they failed in this duty and so it was taken back by the Lord of the Manor around 1874. Lord Hertford then enclosed the ground floor which had always previously been open to the elements, and rented it out; it had been used as the fire station and local court. A Remembrance Day parade, as seen here, is appropriate as the town bought the Hall back from the Marquess in 1919, when it became officially named 'The Memorial Town Hall'.

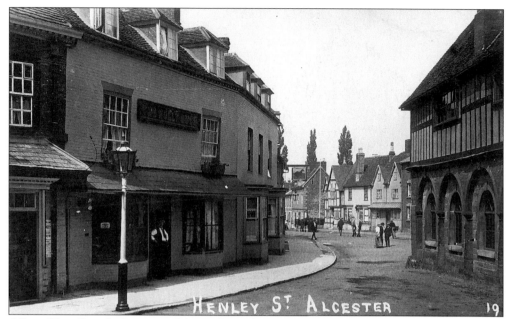

Albert Chandler, the licensee of the Holly Bush, seen in 1916. There is a rumour that a passage existed from the original cellars underneath the road to the former premises of Alcester Brewery.

To the left of the Red Horse, the jettied timber building was formerly another pub called The Greyhound. This lovely general view comes from the very early years of the century, and shows a number of properties which have long since been demolished, notably the ones that can be seen in the middle distance.

The Red Horse inn was converted into residential property late in the 1970s. The current building replaced an earlier inn, known as The Reindeer. The stabling referred to has now been converted to residential use.

The shop opposite the Red Horse was originally run by Joseph Harman as an oil merchant's and general hardware store, as the sign over the door indicates. Here it was being run by his daughter as a sweet and grocery shop, called Wilkes', which closed in the early 1970s.

This is probably Mrs Wilkes standing at the door of the shop. She appears ready to do business with some willing customers, who will have probably been bribed by the photographer with the promise of sweets. Note the flagpole lower down the street, outside what was then the police station.

Both of the buildings to the centre of this picture, Nos. 32–34 and 36–38, are occupied as two separate dwellings divided by a central passageway. The meat from the ox roast would be taken into the Red Horse where the ox dinners would be sold.

The Fourt family were bakers as we have seen earlier, and in the middle of the nineteenth century they opened the Bakers Arms. It had a very poor reputation at the start of the century, when objections to its licence being renewed were made and it finally closed in 1923. Next door is probably the oldest property in the town, which was of cruck construction.

Another view of the 1924 flood, showing that the more recent alterations to School Road and the properties that have been built there have actually reduced the level of flooding, which still occurs regularly. The cottages opposite Frank Dyson's grocer's at No. 1 Henley Street were known as Spring Gardens.

Oversley House was constructed in 1837, specifically as a workhouse, serving parishes including Studley and Inkberrow. The building has now been converted into privately owned sheltered housing for the elderly. As a workhouse it replaced the Rookery in Stratford Road, and was used regularly by tramps until 1940.

Approximately opposite Oversley House, the Hertford Memorial Sanatorium was built as a memorial to the fifth Marquess of Hertford who died in 1884. The house was the residence of the matron, but there were often no patients. This was a hospital for people suffering from contagious diseases and Bob Buggins recalled spending more than ten weeks here with scarlet fever.

Alcester Hospital was built to the rear of Oversley House in 1910, and originally served as an infirmary for the workhouse. The Voluntary Aid Detachment took over the hospital during the war. The VAD was made up of ladies from the aristocracy, universities and generally good families. Many of them had never worked, prior to the Great War, but there were very few trained professional nurses at that time, and the ladies of the VAD filled this requirement.

Although now occupied by corporate offices, the building in the distance was, within the memory of many Alcester folk, the venue of Kinwarton preparatory school. Many people have, over the years, told me that they started their education here under the headship of Philip Rutter.

Six
A Local Selection

This is presumably the postmistress, Clara Martha Edwards, at Great Alne post office, c. 1910. She was a most respected lady of the village, and acted as postmistress until 1954, when she was aged seventy-seven. Great Alne was actually built on the 'great road' from London to Shrewsbury and Holyhead in the seventeenth century, when coaches dropped the Birmingham mail at the Mother Huff Cap.

Even at the turn of the century the level of the road through Wixford was considerably lower than that of the cottages shown here. It gives a clear impression of the origin of the current address, 'The Bank'.

Hidden in the ivy over the fireplace, inside the tap room of the Fish Inn, Wixford, is an interesting advertisement for the ales and stouts from Alcester Brewery.

Mrs Cheape, 'The Squire of Bentley', and her harriers are about to set out hare hunting. She was the daughter of the Hemmings of Bentley Manor, near Redditch. The family made its fortune in the needle industry, and her father had liked the Haselor area so much that he bought most of it.

Haselor's second post office was renovated by Mrs Cheape for Mr and Mrs Oliver Leach. At this time there were two deliveries of post a day in the village. The tree opposite fell across the road on 28 March 1916, seriously damaging the building.

Many postcards were printed for advertising and communication purposes by both national and local firms. In some cases, common views were overprinted on the rear with advertising material. However, in this case Bomford's are using their own card which they printed as being sent from Exhall Court, Alcester. It was sent to advise a Mr Langston at Ardens Grafton that 'your plough is ready'.

The sender of this card describes Dunnington as, 'just the sort of place which would suit you and Stanley together for a month or so'.

Sambourne was one of the first centres of the local needle trade and is mentioned in the Domesday Book. The manor was part of the original endowment of Evesham Abbey. Here, Edgar Somers was licensee of The Green Dragon. Note that the two boys to the left have been playing the traditional hoop.

The opportunity for a photograph like this would have had all of the Redditch photographers on the scene. This picture must have been taken several days after the storm as the tree had crashed down pretty well intact.

Perhaps somebody will be inspired by this early photograph to compile a similar book for Studley. The rather sad message is 'there is only two little girls left here now but I am better now I get letters'.

I make no excuse for including one of my favourite photographs, although it is somewhat outside our area. This is the original structure of the Dog Inn, although many will remember it when it had been extended to the right. Inside, it was hardly altered from the early years of the century. The building was later demolished to make way for the new Dog.

Seven
Ragley Park

RAGLEY GATES

Much of Alcester was sold by the Earl family of Warwick, to the Seymour family of Ragley Hall at the beginning of the nineteenth century. The final sale in 1813 included the rights of the manor, although by that time these were only nominal. The involvement of the Seymour family within the town was much greater then than it is today, and they donated or made land available for the local good. Many earlier photographs also show that Ragley Park itself was widely used for a number of purposes, whether military, recreational, social or otherwise. In particular the Park was an important camping venue for the Royal Warwickshire Regiment from the first decade of this century until the 1930s. Postcards of the Park from this era are fairly easily obtainable, because so many would have been printed for use by the members of the Regiment. Cards by the local photographer W.H. Smith are most prolific but I have seen examples by L.L. Sealey of Redditch as well as national publishers. There is also a set of six cards by the Lewis Brothers dating from around 1906. They are individually numbered and comprise of various views of the Hall itself, except for No. 1, which is a picture of the two lodges. The lodges, at the main entrance to Ragley Park, were erected in the 1780s. Originally a single storey building, a floor was added to form a bedroom which was served by two circular swivel-opening lights. The lodge to the left is still occupied today, although it has been extended to the rear to provide modern facilities.

PRINCESS LOUISE OF HOLSTEIN OPENING BAZAAR AT RAGLEY PARK 27 6 08

The neatness of the caption would suggest that it was not produced by one of the local photographers who invariably used freehand writing, which often led to spelling errors and reversed letters.

Official postcards were printed in vast quantities for use by the military and in this case the insignia has been embossed. The design layout originated from a time when the message had to be written on the front of the card with the address only, on the reverse.

This picture gives some idea of the vast numbers of soldiers who attended the military camps at Ragley Hall and here locals are clearly welcome to witness the spectacle. The Yeomanry merged into the Territorial Army in 1907. This rather poor quality mass produced printed picture was published by the Mezzotint Company of Brighton.

In the early days of aviation, air shows were very popular and during the course of such a show held at Stratford; this pilot flew to Ragley Park attracting huge crowds.

I cannot help but contrast the lengthy procession shown in the many photographs of the funeral of the Marquess of Hertford on 26 March 1912, with that of the Marquess which the town witnessed in the early part of 1998. Here local dignitaries precede the carriages of members of the aristocracy to the church at Arrow.

WAR. VOL. RIFLE CORPS CAMPING AT RAGLEY PARK.

The bell tents would 'house' six to eight men during their stay at camp and the marquees to the right were the mess tents. The message on the card indicates that a local deer showed great interest in the men at drill.

Each Regiment had a mascot for ceremonial occasions, and the choice of a goat was relatively common.

Everyone at camp would be expected to join in what would be extremely competitive sporting activity. There would be no exception for those less suited to football or the like.

Ragley Hall was graced by the visit of Queen Mary, who is seen here, sitting with the family and her ladies in waiting.

The opening of the bandstand in the recreation ground. Those present include: Lord Hertford with Lady Helen and Lady Margaret, Stuart Wright, Alf Redding, George Wilkes, Freddie Stringman, Arthur Wilkes, Eric Bunting, Mrs Bunting, Ernest Walker, Revd Andrews and George Haines.

Eight
Groups, Clubs
and Teams

This is one of the first official portraits of the new Alcester grammar school. There are younger pupils present because at this time a preparatory school was incorporated. The headmaster is Mr E. Wells. The photographer was Arthur Clarke who ran his Windsor Portrait Gallery from Evesham Street, in Redditch, and is known to have produced hundreds of very high quality views of Redditch and district.

A number of children were evacuated into Alcester from the Blitz of Coventry and were accommodated at Oversley House. Father Christmas is thought to be Mr Barton, the matron's husband, and also identified as part of the group are: Stuart Wright, Kay Collins, Evelyn Wright and Mary Ison.

Mr Collins, on the back row second from the left, was headmaster of the Alcester National School from 1923. He is seen here with staff who are, on the back row, from left to right: Eva Payne (pupil teacher), Miss Parkinson, Mr Towler, and Mrs Allchurch. On the front row: Miss Gibbs, Miss Reading, Miss Thornley and Miss Morris.

This 1938 mixed schools group photograph was taken in the field opposite the National School in School Road. I confidently expect someone to be able to name every pupil, but as a start on the seated row, third from the left is Iris Daffern and on the front row, third from left is Josephine Lewis.

A church party at the Town Hall. At the front is 'Arthur's Harem', who were: the hairdresser Arthur Keyte with Mary Baylis, Janet Clark, Hilda Ankcorn, Edna Ison and Iris Ison. Also identified, in the middle row are: Stan Baylis, Evelyn Wright, Miss Adcock, Charles Guillaume, Dorothy Fancote, Celia Chapman, Jim Adcock and Stuart Wright.

The Roman Catholic school was run for all ages, in only two rooms, in Priory Road from 1902, and there was no electricity until 1939. Identified in the back row are: fifth from the right, Ray Keyte; sixth, Ron Gregory; and ninth, Vera Keyte.

Most towns and all cities had companies of the Church Lads Brigade or the Boys Brigade, which were linked to one of its churches and a church parade would take place on a regular monthly basis.

In 1897, the Alcester town band was formed specifically to play in Queens Victoria's Diamond Jubilee procession; previously, bands had been brought in from other towns. Mr Collins was then the bandmaster. By King Edwards VII's coronation the name of the band had been changed to the Victoria Brass Band and is now of course called the Victoria Silver Band.

The band was, and remains, an important section within such youth organizations as the Boys Brigade or, as seen here, the local Church Lads Brigade. Charlie Dowdswell can be seen seated second on the right of the base drum.

School sports day, around 1928. On the back row are: Miss Redding, Mr Collins (headmaster), Miss Vale, Mr Cook and Mr Tewlett. Some other names identified are: ? Tarver, ? Allchurch, Ruth Richardson, George Wheatley, Sam Styler, ? Fletcher, Beryl Elliker, Ken Collins, Muriel Canning and Ken Potter.

This team was originally called Alcester Grammar School Old Boys, and kept the town on the map, in football terms between the wars. They were highly successful, winning a number of trophies each year. The goalkeeper standing sixth from the left is Frank Woodfield, the player next to him is G. Keyte.

Members of the Bowls club, in 1938. They include on the back row: John Derby, Charlie Mander, Cyril Hemming and Alfred Crouch. On the middle row: brothers Harry and Len Buggins, and Sam Shepherd. On the front row: Mr Harwood (the Midland bank manager), Mr Hillman (of the Royal Oak) with dog, Mr Gwynett and towards the other end Arthur Baylis.

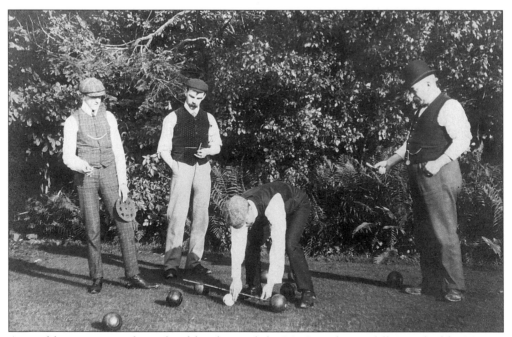

An end being measured at a local bowls match by Mr Crouch, carefully watched by Messers Hunt, Walker and Baylis.

Alcester acquired its first steam driven fire engine in 1902, with part of the cost being raised by the brigade itself and the balance being made up by way of mortgage. The appliance was horsedrawn. This picture was almost certainly taken for advertising purposes on behalf of the manufacturers and was published by the Halifax Photographic Company.

Joe Baylis, looking every inch the bookmaker, attended this Autumn meeting at Sandown Park Racecourse. His assistant keeping the book is Josh Hunt.

Nine

Events and Celebrations

ALCESTER JUNE 22 /11

On special occasions such as coronations, royal jubilees, peace celebrations and the like, the people of Britain would, within their own communities, dress in their finest clothes, and decorate the streets with flags and bunting. They would join in processions, street games, meals, presentations and dancing. While the emphasis would inevitably be within High Street, many photographs show Bleachfield Street and Malt Mill Lane when they were liberally festooned. We start with the Coronation of King George V when the High Street saw a number of races and other events during the course of the day. Entry was only allowed for inhabitants of Alcester and Kinwarton. Eighteen tables were erected for a 'meat tea' which was provided for adults. The children were looked after in Church Street, and this is a practice which seems to have prevailed through a number of celebrations. The children were each given a coronation mug. There was a torch-lit procession later in the day led by the bailiffs who were followed by Alcester's Victoria Brass Band and the fire brigade. The captain of the fire brigade, George Haines had ensured that posters had been placed throughout the town in the preceding a week, warning about the danger of fire in the following terms: 'With a view of preventing, as far as possible, any outbreak of Fire on the evening of the 22nd instant, may I respectfully ask that the Inhabitants of Alcester, who are illuminating their Windows on the inside, to be careful to be place all Curtains and Blinds beyond reach of any light or lights'.

Here we see the decorations in Malt Mill Lane for the Coronation of George VI, when the king's speech was actually broadcast in High Street. The ladies in overalls, to the right, are sisters Elsie and Doris Fletcher.

The official opening of a traditional English garden party in the Rectory garden. Various side-shows and stalls can be seen in the background.

The Allies were still technically at war with the Central Powers until the signing of the Treaty of Versailles in July 1919, and although many triumphal processions had taken place after the armistice, it was not until 19 July that the official celebrations took place throughout the nation. There was a huge victory march of troops and tanks in London. As ever Alcester's day would start with a church service, which on this occasion was held, at least partly, outdoors.

Following the pattern that had been taken up for previous coronation celebrations, races of all kinds were held in High Street during the afternoon and here we see what appears to be the start of the egg and spoon race.

It seems that the children were always given tea in Church Street. On the table, the tea urn appears as a traditional samovar and the victory mugs which the children were given are plainly in use. Margaret Crouch can be seen at the corner of the table.

Pageants were popular throughout the country during the first forty or so years of the twentieth century and all were recorded in postcard form. They would have a specific theme or purpose and were similar in format to the carnivals which we know today. To celebrate the peace, there were groups representing each of the Allied countries and here we see those for Australia and New Zealand.

The old Corn Exchange in the High Street, before it became the cinema, was hired out for many general purposes in the way of meetings, entertainment, lectures and the like. Inevitably the circus became extremely popular, a craze that started with Buffalo Bill's Circus before the First World War, but on Monday 4 April 1921, Alcester had one belonging to Sir R. Fossett.

It was not uncommon for a war memorial to have its ceremony of dedication some years after the end of the First World War. The design and siting of such a memorial had to be agreed upon and more importantly funds had to be raised to meet the cost of construction.

Gardens fêtes were frequently held at the Rectory during the 1920s and 1930s. The children do not seem to be too enthralled with the fancy dress competition. Most of the costumes are made from crêpe paper.

This is a group photograph from the same garden fête. On the back row, second from the left is Margaret Crouch and on the middle row, fourth from the left is Marjorie Mander of Castle House, Butter Street, whose mother always arranged the refreshments at these events.

Local businesses were quite willing to lend suitable transport for the pageant or carnival parades.

A float representing the founding of the Benedictine Abbey at Alcester by Ralph Boteler around 1140. The Abbey was sited close to Ragley Mill.

The telephone number on the side of this lorry identifies it as belonging to Alcester Builders. Although there are no specific clues, this picture of the 1929 Peace Pageant could be dated by making reference to the style of clothes worn by the watching ladies to the front and rear, in particular the hats.

The rather peculiar hats denote members of Alcester Jazz Band formed by Cyril 'Ziggy' Davis, in the 1930s. As well as the ukulele towards the front, we see the gentleman in the centre picture holding a kazoo.

The whole town was in holiday mood for the Silver Jubilee festivities in May 1935. The day started with a huge procession of the various town bands, youth groups, police, bailiffs and the fire brigade, interspersed with the townspeople. The bells were ringing to herald the church service.

Alcester Ladies Jazz Band at the Jubilee. On the back row, first from the left is Mary Hayward, second is Beryl Truman and sixth is Rose Beech. Third from right is Dora Fennemore.

During the afternoon there were many events including races in the High Street and the fancy dress competition.

There was an official programme for the day, selling at two pence, detailing such other events as the baby show, slow bicycle race, pram race, tug-of-war and even a bun eating competition. Prizes were as much as fifteen shillings.

Anyone working or living in the town for any length of time would not forget the local window cleaner and great character, Tommy Jones. Here he can be seen seated towards the front, facing the camera. The gentleman behind him, holding the jug, is said to be Ted Broadly.

The 'lady' in bed is actually Arthur Keyte. Reg and Muriel Grummett can be seen just in the picture to the right with Olive and Bill Vernon in the centre. Arthur Rippington can be seen over Bill Vernon's shoulder.

The Flintstones appear to have gatecrashed the coronation procession.

Harry Strain steadies the horse for the camera, closely watched by members of the local fire brigade, who were waiting to continue with the procession.

Another picture of the coronation procession. In the watching crowd, with his hands in his pockets, is Arthur Payne. The tall man to the left, with the banded trilby hat, is Reg Morgan, known locally as 'Long Tom'.

The 1911 coronation, once more. The procession had started at the Town Hall and then continued into Henley Street, School Road, Priory Road and High Street on its way to the church. Note the portraits of King George and Queen Mary between the first floor windows at Bunting's Stores, and the Venetian mast with a shield, bearing the royal initials.

Services were held at both the parish and Catholic churches, which were preceded by the usual processions. Note the mast and shield mentioned earlier.

A Second World War church parade, with the ambulance drivers, Red Cross and civil nursing reserves. Among the shops can be seen the printing works at which the *Alcester Chronicle* was published, Keyte's newsagent's and Stanley's ironmongers.

Another church parade, this time in August 1942. Among the nurses are Miss Thompson, Miss Machin and Miss Aston.

Mr Collins, the headmaster, is seen here at the ceremony for the unveiling of the Town Hall plaque in 1938. The standard bearer is Albert Spires with Mr Tanner, and Fireman Dyson can be seen standing on the left of the picture.

The Mop was a traditional recruitment fair at which those seeking work could make their availability and particular calling known to employers. This role ceased in the late nineteenth century; since then the Mop has been a commercial fair with street entertainment.

Many photographs of the 1910 Mop survived because side shows and the roasting of an ox were reinstated for the first time in this year.

Another picture of the folk of Alcester, at the 1910 Mop, this time viewing the ox roast to the front of the church. At No. 3 High Street, Mrs Blunn's shop was selling stationery and fancy goods.

The Mop in 1934. The billiards tent was positioned by the Royal Oak and standing in the centre of the picture, with folded arms, is Walter Lamb. The babe in arms to the left held by his grandmother Annie Keyte, is the old silver fox himself, Derek Malin aged three months.

Alfred Crouch, who was known as 'Bobby', selling clockwork toys at an as yet unknown venue. The nickname 'Bobby' is a reference to his dapper style of dressing as 'Bobby Dazzler'.

This traditional mobile ice-cream handcart belonged to Jack Herdman. He also supplied some of the shops in the town centre.

The dress of 100 pockets was worn first by Mrs Hunt, then by Nellie Danks, to many fund raising events. Here it is seen at a garden party at the Rectory.

A rare ginger beer bottle. From 1822, the Overbury family ran the Angel Inn at 4–5 Church Street and it is known that the inn had its own brewery, as the brewing vessels are mentioned in the will of Richard Overbury.

Acknowledgements

I would like to thank those not mentioned elsewhere, who have loaned photographs or postcards. Firstly, I would like to thank the daughters of the late Margaret Rees, Dylis and Bronwen, for their kind permission to use photographs from their mother's collection. My thanks are also due to Philip Coventry whose companion volume on Redditch is recommended. Thank you to Chris Jones and of course Suzanne Goode, shortly to start her twenty-fourth year as my secretary. Special thanks to Derek Malin for so many of his family photographs and his knowledge of their background. Recognition is due to my personal staff Suzanne, Julie, Chris, Angela and especially Sandra Calverley who has been responsible for the preparation and presentation of the written material contained within. My final and perhaps most important thanks go to Lynn for putting up with so many hours of disruption to the household and suffering my pictures, postcards, books, tapes and notes littering our lounge and dining room for so many months.

Comic postcards were produced in vast numbers in Edwardian times, although they were mainly published for the seaside holiday market. Many designs were mass-produced, with captions which could be completed locally with the name of a town being overprinted as in this case.